Employee Engagement for Everyone

4 Keys to Happiness and Fulfillment at Work

First Edition

NY Times Bestselling Author

Kevin Kruse

www.kevinkruse.com

Personal Message from Kevin Kruse

Hello! I love writing books, but what I love even more is connecting with readers. I hope you'll reach out to introduce yourself and share what you're working on or struggling with these days.

I also invite you to join my mailing list so you can get exclusive free content and information on future books and speaking engagements. To get in touch, visit: http://www.KevinKruse.com.

Bulk Purchases and Speaking

For information on discounts for bulk purchases, or to invite Kevin to speak at your next event, call 267-756-7089 or e-mail info@kevinkruse.com.

www.KevinKruse.com

ISBN: 978-0-9850564-2-1
First printing: 2013

Table of Contents

◆

Real education is a radical process. It thumps you on the head until everything you know makes no sense anymore.

—Debbie Millman

◆

INTRODUCTION
An Infamous Job Resignation

Many people are unhappy at work. Just ask Steven Slater.

You do remember Steven Slater, don't you?

No?

Here's a hint: A few years ago, there was a JetBlue flight attendant who had a really bad day at work...

Yep, *that* Steven Slater.

It was August 9, 2010, when JetBlue Airways flight attendant Steven Slater decided to quit in spectacular fashion.

The details are in dispute, but apparently Slater had some kind of argument with a passenger, got bonked on the head with a bag in the overhead bin, and just couldn't take it anymore. So when the plane landed at JFK airport in New York, Slater cursed at the passengers over the PA system, grabbed two beers, deployed the evacuation chute, and slid away in what would become the most infamous job resignation in history.

You're probably chuckling right now as you recall the story, but it was actually a very serious incident. The pilots were furious. It turns out that Slater took their last two beers. (Joke shamelessly borrowed from Jay Leno.)

Gallows Humor

"Oh, you hate your job? Why didn't you say so?
There's a support group for that.
It's called everybody, and they meet at the bar."
–Drew Carey (comedian)

What's amazing about the Steven Slater incident isn't what he did. What's amazing is what happened in the aftermath.

The story made headlines around the world. "*Felon? Or working class hero?*" the cable news anchors wanted to know. On social media, Slater trended to the top of Twitter and he gained 182,000 fans in two days on Facebook.

Even though Slater was arrested and eventually pleaded guilty to criminal mischief, many people view Slater as a folk hero who lived out a popular fantasy of stomping off the job in a dramatic fashion.

Slater's crazy antic brought to light the cold hard fact that many, many people are unhappy at work. According to many sources, job satisfaction is at an all-time low.

DID YOU KNOW?

Only 45% of people are "satisfied" with their jobs.

Only 29% are "engaged" at work.

If you aren't fully engaged at work, you're in the majority.

But it doesn't have to be this way.

This short guide is about how you can work as a partner to create a great place to work. It shows you how to increase your own happiness at work, how to take actions that will motivate your colleagues, and how to work with your manager on issues related to employee engagement.

I truly believe that we spend too many hours at work to be anything other than fully engaged in our jobs.

Let's begin!

CHAPTER 1

What is "Engagement" Anyway?

"To find joy in work is to discover
the fountain of youth."
–Pearl S. Buck

OK, first things first. What the heck is "employee engagement" anyway?

Engaged doesn't mean *satisfied*. This is a big misconception. Many companies conduct "employee satisfaction" surveys and loosely talk about employee satisfaction. But being "satisfied" doesn't go far enough. You can be satisfied at work, but that might mean you are satisfied only enough to do the bare minimum to get by. You might be satisfied but still taking calls from recruiters promising a 5% bump in pay. Satisfied isn't enough. And isn't life too short for you to be merely *satisfied* eight or more hours a day?

Engaged doesn't mean *happy*. Of course the leaders in your company *want* you to be happy at work. But just because you're happy, that doesn't necessarily mean that you're focused and working hard towards the goals of the organization. After all, you could be happily hiding in your office playing solitaire on your computer or downloading new apps on your smartphone.

So the question remains: What is employee engagement?

DEFINITION: EMPLOYEE ENGAGEMENT

Employee engagement is the emotional commitment the employee has to the organization and its goals.

This emotional commitment means that engaged employees actually care about their work and their company. They don't work just for a paycheck, or just for the next promotion, but work on behalf of the organization's goals.

When employees care—when they are *engaged*—they use discretionary effort. They go the extra mile.

◆

*When employees care—when they are **engaged**—they use discretionary effort.*

In other words, they are willing to go the extra mile.

◆

ACTIVITY 1.1: Can You See It in Others?

You know how, when you buy a new car, you suddenly notice the same car everywhere? Now that you know about employee engagement, you'll be able to spot it in everyday situations.

It might be the waitress at your favorite restaurant who took the time to learn your name or the grocery bagger who takes extra care not to bruise your fruit. As you go about your normal routine in the week ahead, count the number of times you see people fully engaged in their work.

ACTIVITY 1.2: Can You Feel the Difference?

Now that you know what engagement is and how it differs from satisfaction and happiness, think about your own levels of engagement throughout your career. In what jobs, or at what times, did you find yourself merely satisfied, or even dissatisfied? When have you felt the most engaged and passionate at work?

Use this space to write private notes:

In the next chapter, we'll explore whose job it is to drive engagement.

CHAPTER 2

Engagement: Whose Job Is It?

"The greatest day in your life and mine is when we take total responsibility for our attitudes. That's the day we truly grow up."
—John C. Maxwell

ACTIVITY 2.1: What Do You Think?

Think about a time when you've been engaged or even just satisfied at work. Who do you think should get the credit for that? Where did that satisfaction come from?

Think of a time when you've been dissatisfied at work. Who should take the blame for that? Where did the dissatisfaction come from?

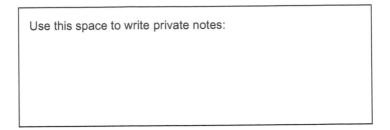

Use this space to write private notes:

As a young man I was once so miserable at work that I quit my job by just walking out the door. Never said a word and never went back.

Later in life I had jobs I loved. Time flew by each day, my manager was great, and I actually looked forward to going to work every Monday.

Later still, I started my own business and, as a boss, hired dozens and eventually hundreds of workers. I can remember the sting and confusion I felt when employees would quit for another opportunity elsewhere.

I took employee departures so seriously that I made creating a great culture my number-one focus, and eventually we won a *Best Place to Work* award—made all the more special because it was based on anonymous surveys of workers.

What I learned from that process—**going from having a bad boss to creating a Best Place to Work**—was that it takes *both* the employee and the manager to create a thriving culture that fosters feelings of full engagement.

♦

It takes two to tango.

(Tango: apparently the official dance of employee engagement!)

♦

Yet, we often look at only half of the equation. "What can the *company* do…? What must *managers* do to increase employee engagement?" Indeed, there is plenty that company leaders need to do to drive engagement.

But the other half of the equation—the other question—is "What can each *individual* do to become fully engaged and to create a great place to work?"

IDG Research did a study that indicates that 57% of how we feel about our jobs comes from external factors that are outside our control, and 43% comes from intrinsic motivation and attitudes that we can control.

DID YOU KNOW?

43% of employee engagement comes from intrinsic motivation (i.e., attitudes that come from inside of you).

Although the ratio of external to internal motivation is not quite 50/50, the study proves the point that (yes) your manager has a role to play, but you as an individual must contribute to your own engagement, too.

In the next chapter, you'll see why it should be important to you to be fully engaged at work.

CHAPTER 3

Why Should *You* Care About Engagement?

"Do something you love and you'll
never work a day in your life."
—*Confucius*

Believe it or not, our jobs affect our physical health, our children, and our relationships. I can remember clearly the best leadership compliment I ever got. It didn't even come from an employee; it came from the wife of someone who worked for me. We were at our annual holiday party when she approached and said, "Before we go, I want to thank you for making my marriage better."

I was confused. I barely knew her and certainly didn't know anything about her marriage!

She continued, "My husband used to come home and be so grumpy I wouldn't even want to be around him. But since he started working for you, he went back to being the man I married."

Wow. He went back to being the man I married. Powerful stuff.

Psychologists refer to the *spillover* and *crossover effects.* Your emotions at work—good or bad—spill over into your personal life, *and even cross over to those around you.*

DID YOU KNOW?

People who are dissatisfied at work weigh on average 5 pounds more than people who are satisfied.

People who are unhappy with their bosses are twice as likely to have a stroke or heart attack.

People who are disengaged at work have less sex than those who are fully engaged.

(Oh, *now* you're paying attention!)

You don't need to be a psychologist to know the effects your job has on your relationships.

If you come home from work in a good mood, you might kiss your spouse hello, make dinner together, and share the day's events over a bottle of wine. That's a night with some possibility!

What about on a bad day? You might come home and grunt hello as you flip through the junk mail. You might grab a beer and plunk down in front of the TV, which is tuned to junk shows. That's probably a night that won't have a lot to offer.

DEFINITIONS

Spillover effect: the positive or negative effects of an individual's working life on their personal life.

Crossover effect: the transfer of positive or negative emotions from an individual to their spouse, or to other family members.

It's the same with our role as a parent. Come home happy and we're more likely to play with our kids, praise them, or help them with their homework.

Come home grumpy or stressed and we shoo our kids away or snap at them. When we reject our children too often or punish them too quickly, they internalize it and express it in the days ahead as either withdrawal or acting out.

When it comes to your health, on a good day you might have the energy to work out, cook a healthy meal, and limit the late-night snacks.

Come home stressed and emotionally drained, and you are more likely to head straight for the couch, seek comfort in a couple of beers, and maybe order a pizza.

THE BIOLOGICAL LINK
BETWEEN STRESS AND EATING

Researchers are finding strong correlations between chronic stress and an increase in appetite. It's been suggested that this goes back to evolutionary times when we developed a biochemical response during frequent "fight or flee" encounters. The hormone, cortisol, triggers appetite to replenish our bodies, but today, since we don't actually have to physically fight or flee, we don't need the extra calories so it ends up being stored as fat.

♦

Want better health?
Become fully engaged at work.

Want a better marriage?
Become fully engaged at work.

Want to be happy in life?

Become fully engaged at work.

♦

Try as you might, you can't just bottle up your emotions at work and leave them behind. If you have any doubt, just ask your partner, kids, and friends if they can tell when you've had a good or bad day at work!

In the next chapter, you'll see why your company wants you to be fully engaged, too.

CHAPTER 4

Why Does Your *Company* Want You to Be Engaged?

"Companies that score highly on engagement have better earnings and fatter margins."
–Gary Hamel

We discussed that engaged employees are emotionally committed to their company's goals, so they are willing to go the extra mile.

It turns out that this extra effort—discretionary effort—has a huge impact on many areas of the business:

- Engaged salespeople give extra effort, so they sell more.

- Engaged customer service representatives give extra effort, so they provide better service.

- Factory workers, software programmers, and all those people who build things give extra effort, so they have higher levels of productivity.

- Quality-control inspectors give extra effort, so products have fewer defects and better quality.

This isn't just theory. Time and again, researchers have shown a strong correlation between engagement and performance results. (For a list of over 30 studies showing the links between engagement and business outcomes, visit www.KevinKruse.com\employee-engagement-research-master-list).

DID YOU KNOW?

Companies with high engagement scores have customer loyalty rates that are two times higher than those of companies with low engagement scores.

All the improvements in sales, service, and productivity inevitably lead to better financial results. In what I call the Engagement-Profit Chain, business drivers fall forward like a series of tumbling dominoes, affecting company growth and profit, which in turn drive higher shareholder returns.

Engaged employees lead to...

higher service, quality, and productivity, leading to...

higher levels of customer satisfaction, leading to...

increased sales (repeat business and referrals), leading to...

higher profit, leading to...

higher shareholder returns.

DID YOU KNOW?

"Engaged" companies have 5x higher total shareholder returns and 6% higher net profit margins than do "non-engaged" companies.

In addition, companies with engaged employees have better employee retention—meaning that fewer people quit to join other companies. That means less money is spent on recruiting new workers and on training and on-boarding new hires.

CASE STUDY: The Campbell Soup Company

Once upon a time, in the year 2000, the Campbell Soup Company was in big trouble.

The company that began in 1869 and sold soup in 120 countries hit a wall. Sales weren't just slowing, they were declining. Campbell lost 54% of their market value in just one year. Campbell's executives were told that their employee engagement levels were the worst ever seen among the Fortune 500.

So the board of directors hired a new CEO, the mild-mannered Douglas Conant, to turn things around.

What do most CEOs do in dire situations?

They might sell off divisions, buy smaller competitors, move into new markets, or maybe even hire investment bankers to evaluate "strategic options."

But that wasn't Doug Conant's style. A *Forbes* magazine article quoted him as saying:

"To win in the marketplace … you must first win in the workplace. I'm obsessed with keeping employee engagement front and center."

So quarter after quarter, year after year, Conant made sure that employee engagement was one of the top initiatives for the Campbell Soup Company.

By 2009, the ratio of engaged employees to disengaged employees reached an astounding **23-to-1**.

More importantly, in the decade that saw the S&P 500 stocks lose 10% of their value, Campbell's stock actually increased by 30%.

In other words, "keeping employee engagement front and center" helped Campbell to achieve **four times greater results for investors**.

So now you can see that employee engagement is the secret ingredient that leads to better business results, including a higher stock price for publicly traded companies.

♦

"To win in the marketplace… you must first win in the workplace. I'm obsessed with keeping employee engagement front and center."

–Doug Conant

♦

◆

The Engagement-Profit chain is the mechanism by which discretionary effort inevitably leads to better business results, including a higher stock price for shareholders.

◆

ACTIVITY 4.1: How Do Profits Affect You?

If you participate in a profit sharing plan, get stock options, or have a 401K that includes stock in your own company, then you directly benefit when your company becomes more profitable.

Even if you aren't directly benefiting, a company's success on the "bottom line" certainly influences bonuses, the size of raises, the ability to re-invest in new projects, and job security for everyone in the company.

Take a couple minutes to think about all the ways that you, too, benefit from your company's profits.

```
Use this space to write private notes:




```

In the next chapter, we'll discuss the four triggers that activate feelings of engagement at work.

CHAPTER 5
What Makes Us *Feel* Engaged?

"Your work is to discover your work,
and then with all your heart to give yourself to it."
–Buddha

OK. Now we're ready to dig in.

We know what engagement is, how it drives amazing business results, and how it affects your health and relationships.

But what makes someone *feel* engaged? (It *is* a feeling.) How do we get people to feel the feeling of engagement?

ACTIVITY 5.1: What Made You Feel Engaged?

Think of a time when you've been fully engaged at work. I hope that's right now, but if it isn't, reflect on all the various jobs you've had and pick a time when you were most engaged.

Now think about these two questions. First, who gets more credit for your engagement: your boss or your company or someone else? Second, what did your company or boss do to help you feel engaged?

Take a couple minutes to think about the source of your feelings of engagement and jot your answers below.

Use this space to write private notes:

When I speak to audiences around the world, I always ask these questions, and the answers are almost always the same. Usually people give the credit to their managers, and sometimes someone will mention that a client or a specific project was the source of his or her engagement.

When I ask what it was about people's relationships with their managers that drove their engagement, I hear comments like: high trust, I felt appreciated, true partnership, she pushed me, she supported me, I was always growing and learning, he was inspirational.

In my *New York Times* bestselling book, *We: How to Increase Performance and Profits Through Full Engagement*, my co-author, Rudy Karsan, and I, detail the drivers of engagement based not just on our own experiences but also on surveys of 10 million workers in 150 countries.

Although there are many drivers of engagement, and each individual can have unique needs, the vast majority of engagement—*how you feel about your job and your work*—comes primarily from four things:

1. Communication — Do you believe that there is frequent, consistent *two-way* communication?

2. Growth and development — Do you believe that you are learning new things and advancing in your career?

3. Recognition and appreciation — Do you feel appreciated?

4. Trust and confidence — Do you trust the leadership and have confidence in your company's future?

We will explore each of these engagement drivers in the chapters ahead.

Numerous research studies also show that engagement is driven primarily by your relationship with your manager. As the saying goes, "People join companies but leave bosses."

This is *so* important! Great managers, through their actions and words, have the ability to magnify the positives and minimize the negatives. Poor managers tend to do the opposite.

◆

Communicate GReAT!

*Remember to **Communicate Growth, Recognition, And Trust.***

◆

So this means that engagement is the boss's job, right?

No!

One of a manager's many responsibilities is to engage her team members. But remember what you learned in Chapter 2. Fifty-three percent of your feelings of engagement comes from what the company controls and what your manager does; the other 47% is your responsibility.

In this chapter we discussed the most common drivers of employee engagement, but each individual is unique. In the next chapter, you'll complete a Personal Engagement Style Profile to discover your most powerful triggers.

CHAPTER 6

What's Your Personal Engagement Style?

"The most important kind of freedom
is to be what you really are."
−Jim Morrison, The Doors

In the powerful book *The 5 Love Languages*, author Gary Chapman asserts that there are five ways that people express or recognize love: with words of affirmation, quality time, gifts, acts of service, and physical touch.

By understanding your own preference for these five signs of love, and the preference of your partner, you can best ensure a feeling of commitment and engagement in the relationship.

As with the "love languages," individuals have different preferences, or triggers, for feelings of engagement at work. Use the profile below to better understand what it takes for *you* to feel fully engaged at work. You can also complete this profile online at kevinkruse.com.

ACTIVITY 6.1: What's Your Engagement Style?

This personal profile consists of 16 statements. Consider each statement and reflect on how much you agree or disagree with its sentiment. Write the number that most closely matches your level of agreement. Remember this scale:

1 = "Strongly Disagree"

2 = "Disagree"

3 = "Neutral"

4 = "Agree"

5 = "Strongly Agree"

COMMUNICATION

_____ Meeting with my manager one-on-one, at least weekly, is important to me.

_____ Meeting with my fellow teammates, at least weekly, is important to me.

_____ I like to read companywide communications, like the annual report or company newsletters.

_____ I like asking questions of my CEO or president during town hall meetings.

GROWTH

_____ Career advancement is important to me.

_____ I like to learn new things and to be challenged at work.

_____ I would like to have a mentor to help guide my career.

_____ Knowing the next steps in my career path is important to me.

RECOGNITION

_____ I feel good when my manager says thank you.

_____ I feel good when a fellow team member says thank you.

_____ I feel good when one of my ideas is implemented at work.

_____ I feel good when someone at work asks for my opinion.

TRUST

_____ Knowing my company's goals is important to me.

_____ I feel good knowing how my work contributes to my company's goals.

_____ It's important to have a manager who cares about me.

_____ It's important that our senior leadership does what it says it will do.

Calculate Your Engagement Style

Add up your scores for the first four questions under the Communication heading, and write the total next to the word "COMMUNICATION" below.

Add up your scores for the second set of questions under the Growth heading, and write the total next to the word "GROWTH" below.

Add up your scores for the third set of questions under the Recognition heading, and write the total next to the word "RECOGNITION" below.

Add up your scores for the final set of four questions under the Trust heading, and write the total next to the word "TRUST" below.

_____ COMMUNICATION

_____ GROWTH

_____ RECOGNITION

_____ TRUST

Interpreting Your Scores

Which engagement driver received your highest score? Circle it above, or write it on a Post-it note and stick it on your computer monitor. This driver is your primary key for unlocking feelings of engagement at work. This is the #1 area for you—and your manager—to focus on in your career.

Do you have a tie, or are several scores close? Each engagement driver can have a score ranging from 4 to 20. Although it's rare, some people have two or more engagement triggers that are tied or several that are just within a point or two of each other. If this is the case for you, consider it a good thing. It means that there is more than one way to trigger your feelings of engagement.

Consider these items to be tools in your engagement toolbox. If one of the four drivers scored much higher than the others, then you want to look for nails to use with that "hammer." But if you have several drivers that scored high, that means you have a hammer, a screwdriver, and a wrench in your engagement toolbox and you'll have many more opportunities to trigger engagement.

Are all your scores 12 or below? If all the drivers have a score of 12 or less, it means that you answered every single question as neutral or with a level of disagreement. You are basically indicating that communication, growth, recognition, and trust aren't important to you. Although this result is very rare, there are other drivers of engagement that turn up less frequently, including teamwork, quality, and corporate responsibility. You should reflect on these items, and any others you can think of, to identify your own engagement triggers.

And if you just can't think of any way you can be fully engaged at work, spend extra time on the last chapter in this book, "Tough Love."

Now let's dive in to explore each engagement driver a little more deeply.

CHAPTER 7

How Can You Improve Communication?

"He who asks a question is a fool for five minutes;
he who does not ask a question
remains a fool forever."
–Chinese proverb

Communication about the "big stuff" and the smaller daily stuff is critical to employee engagement. The big stuff includes the company's mission, vision, values and culture, strategy, and key initiatives.

The smaller stuff, which can be just as important, consists of the things that matter to you on a daily basis. They include communication on work expectations, your projects, performance standards, and your individual performance.

Activity 7.1: How Do You Feel About Communication?

Instructions: Consider each statement below and reflect on how much you agree or disagree with its sentiment. Write the number that most closely matches your level of agreement. Use this scale:

1 = "Strongly Disagree"

2 = "Disagree"

3 = "Neutral"

4 = "Agree"

5 = "Strongly Agree"

_____ I have the information I need to be successful in my job.

_____ My company practices open, honest, and transparent communication.

_____ My company practices regular, two-way communication.

_____ **Total Communication Score**

Calculate Your Total Score

Add up your values for the three questions and write the total next to "Total Communication Score" above.

Interpreting Your Score

A score of 12–15 indicates that you and your company are already doing a great job in the area of communication. A score of 9–12 is good, but indicates that you and your company could do more in this area. A score of 3–9 shows that this is a critical area for you and your company to focus on for improvement.

For employees to feel good about the level of communication in their company, there has to be *two-way* communication.

This is where many managers get it wrong. "What do you mean we need to do a better job of communicating?! We're constantly in meetings and I send out project reports every week!"

These managers need to realize that they need to listen to their team members as often as they are sharing with them.

KEY POINT

Being good at communication means
being good at *two-way* communication!

Activity 7.2: How Does Your Company Communicate?

In the space below or on a separate piece of paper, list all the ways that your company and your manager communicate with you at work. Try to list all the forms of communication, no matter how big or small.

Use this space to write private notes:

Many people don't realize all the different ways their company and managers communicate with them. Look at the list below. How many of these communication tactics does your company use?

1. New-hire orientation and on-boarding

2. Individual meetings

3. Team meetings

4. Companywide meetings (i.e., town hall meetings)

5. Rewards and recognition programs

6. Social and teambuilding events

7. Employee handbook

8. Posters and message boards

9. Company intranet

10. Company website

11. Annual report

12. Company newsletter

13. Letter from the CEO

14. Email updates and alerts

15. Employee opinion surveys

16. Performance reviews

17. Yammer or another enterprise social network

Compare the list above with the list you created for Activity 7.1. Any chance you may have forgotten about some of the efforts your company is making to communicate? Have you been giving your company enough credit for proactive communications?

SAD FACT

64% of Americans say that communication bottlenecks
or a lack of information
negatively affects productivity.

Activity 7.3: How Do *You* Communicate at Work?

In the space below or on a separate piece of paper, list all the ways *you* routinely communicate with your manager, colleagues, and senior leadership at work.

Use this space to write private notes:

Be Proactive on Communication

If you think that two-way communication could be improved where you work, consider talking to your manager about it. She may or may not appreciate your initiative, but you'll never know unless you try.

SAMPLE EMAIL TO MANAGER

Hi Rani,

I'm hoping we can meet one-on-one sometime in the next couple of weeks. I've got some questions and ideas in the area of communication I'd like to run by you.

Can I get a spot on your calendar?

Sample topics you might discuss with your manager:

- The ideal timing of various communications

- The ideal mode of communication (in person, by phone, or by email) for various topics

- Situations in which your manager would like to be cc'd on emails

- The creation of a standard checklist or punchlist of items to review before each project, cycle, or shift

- Recent incidents in which better communication would have saved time or money or improved quality

- The possible benefits of scheduling standing one-on-one meetings

- The possible benefits of scheduling standing department-wide meetings

- The possible implementation of a suggestion box or some other anonymous feedback mechanism

- The status of previously discussed ideas or issues

- The possible benefits of launching or improving the company intranet, newsletter, etc.

- Permission to communicate directly with your boss's boss

- Permission to communicate with clients or with another department or even a competitor

- Progress or roadblocks related to your annual performance goals

Improve Communication by Showing the Way

Effective two-way communication requires a partnership between you and your peers, and between you and your manager. In addition to proactively discussing the topic of communication, you can lead by example and be astonished by the positive effect you'll have on others. Consider the following suggestions:

◆

Usually what we communicate isn't the problem; it's what we don't communicate that is.

◆

1. <u>Make it a habit to be the first to ask a question in a group setting</u>—Many people have questions in team meetings but aren't comfortable going first. Help your colleagues out and break the ice with "I think many people might be wondering…"

2. <u>If you are wondering, ask</u>—It's not fair to complain about not getting information if you had the chance to ask for it and didn't.

3. <u>Confirm understanding</u>—If you are sharing information with an individual or a team, make sure to ask if everything is clear and ask if anyone has any questions.

4. <u>Maintain good body language</u>—Maintain eye contact and a forward posture, and nod when you agree with something.

5. <u>Be clear and brief when speaking</u>—Effective communication includes not wasting anybody's time; you will receive more attention when people know that what you say is going to count.

6. <u>Share what you discover</u>—If you fill a knowledge hole through some research or a conversation with your manager, share it with your peers (the odds are, they have the same questions you do).

In the next chapter, we'll dive deeper into the topics of growth, learning, and development.

CHAPTER 8
How Can You Drive Growth?

"I don't think much of a man who
is not wiser today than he was yesterday."
—*Abraham Lincoln*

While it's nice to get a promotion, along with the better title and compensation that come with it, for most people it's the week-to-week feeling of *growing on the inside* that counts most.

Activity 8.1:
Do You Believe that You Are Growing?

Instructions: Consider each statement below and reflect on how much you agree or disagree with its sentiment. Write the number that most closely matches your level of agreement. Use this scale:

1 = "Strongly Disagree"

2 = "Disagree"

3 = "Neutral"

4 = "Agree"

5 = "Strongly Agree"

_____ I can accomplish my career goals at my company.

_____ My company enables me to learn new things and to develop new skills.

_____ My work is interesting and challenging.

_____ **Total Growth Score**

Calculate Your Total Score

Add up your values for the three questions and write the total next to "Total Growth Score" above.

Interpreting Your Score

A score of 12–15 indicates that you and your company are already doing a great job in the area of growth and development. A score of 9–12 is good, but indicates that you and your company could do more in this area. A score of 3–9 shows that this is a critical area for you and your company to focus on for improvement.

For you to be emotionally committed to your company and its goals, it's likely that you need to advance and learn new things.

Activity 8.2: How Does Your Company Support Your Growth and Development?

In the space below, list the ways that your company offers opportunities for career growth and learning.

```
Use this space to write private notes:




```

Many people don't recall all the ways their company fosters growth and development in the workforce.

1. Workshops offered by the in-house training and development department

2. Online e-learning (i.e., a "virtual university")

3. Tuition reimbursement for outside college courses

4. Opportunities to attend outside conferences and seminars

5. Mentoring initiatives

6. Executive coaching

7. Job rotations

8. Career path or talent management software systems

9. Personality assessments (e.g., MBTI, DiSC)

10. Business books

11. Lunch-and-learn programs

12. Internal job postings

13. Team-building activities

14. Experiential opportunities (i.e., a variety of projects or assignments designed to help you gain new experiences)

How many of these items does your company provide? Did you forget to include some of these items in the list you created for Activity 8.2? Have you been giving enough credit to your company for all the things it is doing to facilitate growth, learning, and development?

Be Proactive on Growth

If you aren't growing or developing to your satisfaction, talk to your manager about it.

SAMPLE EMAIL TO MANAGER

```
Hi Jane,

I've been thinking about my career path and
areas I should focus on for further
development. I'd love your perspective and
guidance.

Could we meet one-on-one sometime in the
next couple of weeks to discuss?
```

Consider talking to your manager every six months about your career path. Things you might discuss:

- Share your 3- to 5-year career goals.

- Ask your manager if your goals seem reasonable.

- Ask your manager if she would envision a different career path for you based on your strengths and experience.

- Ask what kinds of knowledge, skills, experiences, and relationships you need to build in order to reach your goals.

- Ask your manager to keep you in mind for any unique projects or opportunities that you could be assigned to so you can develop new skills.

- Ask your manager what kinds of learning opportunities you might be able to take advantage of in the year ahead.

- Ask how many days away from normal work you might be able to use for learning opportunities.

- Ask if there is a budget you should keep in mind for learning opportunities.

Become a Lifelong Learner

Although your growth at work should indeed be viewed as a partnership between you and your employer, ultimately you should develop a "lifelong learning" mindset, regardless of your career situation.

Long gone are the days when most people would join one company for life. Due to the dynamics of global business competition, and primarily because of the rate of technology change, we all must be lifelong learners in order to stay current with the times and relevant in the job market.

Continuing education in the pursuit of a higher degree, along with formal training opportunities, is almost certainly worthwhile. However, just as important—*maybe more important*—is to keep up to speed with current industry developments and to keep your skills relevant for today's employers.

For example, if you work in the finance department of a major pharmaceutical company, you want to stay current with the latest developments in both the life sciences industry *and* accounting. If you are a sales professional in a software company, you should constantly be learning new things about selling *and* the IT industry.

Here are 10 sources you can learn from every day that don't cost a lot of money.

1. Trade and professional magazines

2. Blogs

3. Podcasts

4. Conferences and seminars

5. Trade associations

6. YouTube

7. LinkedIn News

8. Public radio

9. Online learning

10. Books

◆

We all must become lifelong learners to remain relevant in the job market.

◆

◆

*"I have never let my schooling
interfere with my education."*
−Mark Twain

◆

A Daily Ritual for Growth

Many decades ago—or at least in the 1950s TV version of life in middle-class America—people would start their day with coffee, breakfast, and the morning paper.

Today, for many people, Facebook has replaced the morning paper. Facebook offers news personalized and tailored just for you—the pictures of cats and funny babies, the witty cartoons, and of course the crazy and cool stuff your friends did since you last checked into Facebook.

While there's nothing wrong with staying socially connected, I'd encourage you to use your morning coffee time to fuel up your brain first.

Scan the world news headlines, read blog posts from industry leaders, log into LinkedIn, and read relevant group posts and make new connections. If you really care about growth, you can always eat lunch at your desk while doing further reading or taking e-learning courses.

In the next chapter, we'll explore the power of recognition and appreciation.

CHAPTER 9

How Can You Help with Recognition?

"If the only prayer you ever say in your entire life is thank you, it will be enough."
—Meister Eckhart

Recognition is a critical way for you to feel *appreciated* and valued at work. While awards and rewards are two ways to provide recognition, the most powerful form of recognition is usually a sincere "thank you" from a boss or co-worker.

In a survey of more than 1,000 executives, managers, and employees, *McKinsey Quarterly* found that "praise and commendation from immediate managers" and "attention from leaders" were the top two incentives for motivating employees.

Activity 9.1: Do You Feel Appreciated?

Instructions: Consider each statement below and reflect on how much you agree or disagree with its sentiment. Write the number that most closely matches your level of agreement. Use this scale:

1 = "Strongly Disagree"

2 = "Disagree"

3 = "Neutral"

4 = "Agree"

5 = "Strongly Agree"

_____ I feel appreciated at work.

_____ People who go "above and beyond" normal requirements are recognized by my company.

_____ People who get outstanding results are recognized by my company.

_____ **Total Recognition Score**

Calculate Your Total Score

Add up your values for the three questions and write the total next to "Total Recognition Score" above.

Interpreting Your Score

A score of 12–15 indicates that you and your company are already doing a great job in the area of recognition. A score of 9–12 is good, but indicates that you and your company could do more in this area. A score of 3–9 shows that this is a critical area for you and your company to focus on for improvement.

Activity 9.2: How Does Your Company Recognize Employees?

In the space below, list all the ways your company recognizes employees (shows appreciation).

Use this space to write private notes:

Many people don't recall all the different ways their company shows appreciation. Look at the list below. How many of these items are offered by your company?

1. Saying "thank you"

2. Handwritten thank-you notes

3. Comp time

4. Free lunch or special meals

5. Employee-of-the-month awards

6. President's high achiever club

7. Gift for a certain number of years of service (tenure)

8. Company holiday parties

9. Company picnics

10. Online recognition system (typically, anyone can award points or thank a colleague; points accumulate through the year)

11. End-of-the-year bonus

How many of these items does your company practice? Did you forget to include some of these items in the list you created for Activity 9.2? Any chance you weren't giving credit to your company for all the ways it is already recognizing employees?

SAD FACT

Only 10% of adults say thank you
to a colleague each day.

Only 7% express gratitude to a boss.

Be Proactive on Recognition

If you think that more can be done to make yourself and your colleagues feel appreciated, use your own actions to change the culture.

The easiest and most powerful thing you can do is to thank others. As long as you do it sincerely, and only when it's deserved, you can never thank people enough. You'll notice that the people you thank will begin to thank you, too, when you've done something they appreciate. Creating a culture of peer-to-peer appreciation begins with your own actions.

Similar to the way people craft great thank-you notes for gifts, thank-you's at work should consist of three parts:

1. Say thanks.

2. Mention the behavior or achievement.

3. Tie it back to a clear benefit.

And remember that thanks can be sincere, but also fun. Examples of three-part thank-you's:

- "Claire, thanks for working a double shift tonight. I would have been buried on this register without you."

- "Morri, just wanted to thank you for helping me out with Excel earlier this week. Macros are my weakness, but you helped me to finish up before 5pm. Much appreciated!"

- "Nigel, great job on landing that monster deal. Your sales mean job security for me for another year!"

If you think the company or your manager could be doing more to foster a culture of appreciation, simply bring up your ideas to your boss.

SAMPLE EMAIL TO MANAGER

Hi Ramit,

I was thinking about the employee engagement training we recently completed, and I have some ideas for how we can create a culture of recognition and appreciation.

```
Would love to get your thoughts and perspec-
tive. Can we meet briefly to discuss or
continue chatting via email?
```

Ideas for how you might have a conversation with your manager:

- "Ramit, not sure if you noticed, but Anne was cranking out code past midnight last night. Just wanted to make sure you knew how much she did to help us hit that deadline..."

- "Ramit, I was thinking maybe we could set up a gratitude box where people could put slips of paper thanking team members for great effort or achievements. We could draw names randomly for special recognition or some kind of prize. What do you think of that idea?"

- "Ramit, I was thinking we could all benefit from an employee-of-the-month program. Do you have any budget for something cheap like a pizza party or even a token gift to give to the winner?"

- "Just curious if you've ever nominated anyone from our department for the President's Award?"

- "What would someone have to do, or achieve, for you to consider nominating someone for the President's Award?"

◆

Campbell Soup CEO
Doug Conant wrote 20 thank-you notes by hand at the end of each day.

That's over 30,000 notes in nine years!

◆

30 Low-Cost Ways to Thank Colleagues

1. A sincere word of thanks costs nothing and is very effective.

2. Post a thank-you note on the person's door.

3. Throw a pizza party or cake party in the person's honor.

4. Create a simple "ABCD" card that is given when someone goes "Above and Beyond the Call of Duty."

5. Write about colleagues in a company-wide email message.

6. Give a long lunch, an extra break, or comp time.

7. Honor colleagues at the start of the next staff meeting (or recognize someone at the start of every staff meeting).

8. In the lobby, post a "thank you" sign with the person's name on it.

9. Give colleagues flowers, a book, or some other small gift.

10. Invite colleagues to a one-on-one lunch.

11. Give them a card with lottery tickets inside.

12. Give them a card with movie tickets inside, or better yet, take them to a matinee.

13. Give them a card with a Starbucks gift certificate.

14. Have the entire team sign a framed photo or certificate of appreciation.

15. Arrange for a boss several levels up to stop by to say thanks.

16. Send a thank-you note or gift basket to the person's spouse.

17. Arrange to have the person's car washed.

18. Arrange to have the person's home cleaned.

19. Let people bring their pets to work.

20. Buy a dozen donuts and announce to the department that they are in the honorees' office, and people should stop by to say hi and get one.

21. Feature colleagues in the company newsletter.

22. Pick an unusual or funny object and place it on the person's desk for a week.

23. Let people dress casually for a day.

24. Have the entire team honor the person with a standing ovation at the start of the next staff meeting.

25. Offer to swap a task with the person for a day or a week.

◆

Make it a habit to tell people thank you. To express your appreciation, sincerely and without the expectation of anything in return.
–Ralph Marston

◆

26. Pay for spouse to accompany employee on a business trip

27. Unexpectedly bring the person a cup of coffee or their favorite snack.

28. Arrange for a limo to drive the employee to work for a day or week.

29. Temporarily name a conference room after the honored employee; put their picture on the wall.

30. Invite the employee to attend a sales call, client meeting or even board meeting as an observer.

In the next chapter, we'll explore the notion of trusting our leaders and having confidence that we'll achieve our collective goals.

CHAPTER 10

How Can You Help Build Trust?

"It's a terrible thing to see and have no vision."
–Helen Keller

Activity 10.1: Do You Trust Your Leadership?

Instructions: Consider each statement below and reflect on how much you agree or disagree with its sentiment. Write the number that most closely matches your level of agreement. Use this scale:

1 = "Strongly Disagree"

2 = "Disagree"

3 = "Neutral"

4 = "Agree"

5 = "Strongly Agree"

_____ I trust our organization's leaders.

_____ I'm confident that our company will achieve its goals.

_____ I'm confident that our leaders will overcome our current challenges.

_____ **Total Trust Score**

Calculate Your Total Score

Add up your values for the three questions and write the total next to "Total Trust Score" above.

Interpreting Your Score

A score of 12–15 indicates that you and your company are already doing a great job in the area of trust. A score of 9–12 is good, but indicates that you and your company could do more in this area. A score of 3–9 shows that this is a critical area for you and your company to focus on for improvement.

Trust in leadership is the foundation for all engagement. However, it isn't really ethics that we're talking about. Being honest and ethical are certainly the low bars we must all step over, but it's actually quite rare for people to think that their company leaders are actively lying, cheating, or breaking the law.

SAD FACT

In 2012, CEO credibility declined 12 points to 38%, its biggest drop in 9 years.

What you really need is to trust that your leaders are going to guide you to a brighter future. It's really about having *confidence* that you collectively are heading in the right direction and will eventually get there.

Let's be crystal clear here. To trust the future—*to have confidence in the future*—you need to know what your company's goals are and have at least a vague idea of how you're going to get there.

In *Built to Last*, authors Jim Collins and Jerry Porras describe the power of a medium- to long-term goal to focus everyone in an organization on a common future. For this goal, typically set five or more years in the future, Collins and Porras coined the term "Big Hairy Audacious Goal," or "BHAG" (pronounced bee-hag) for short.

Take, for example, a company known around the globe, the Coca-Cola Company. You know that Coca-Cola must have a massive strategic plan. They operate in over 200 countries, carry more than 3,500 brands, and have 700,000 employees. Their operating plan certainly has quarterly targets, annual objectives, and medium-term goals. If printed, their plan must fill reams and reams of paper.

Yet Coca-Cola has boiled down their BHAG to this: **2020 Vision**.

That's it: "2020 Vision."

But what it means is that they plan to double revenues (20, 20) by the year 2020.

Now if you want to poke on their plan further, the company will explain that it's built on the six P's: Profit, People, Portfolio, Partners, Planet, and Productivity. Dig deeper and you'll find a one-page summary. Dig deeper still and you can get to their massive plan. But the point is this...

Every single Coca-Cola employee knows and remembers "2020 Vision." They have a memorable picture of growth, a brighter future, a goal. Even if any given year throws them a challenge, they know their leaders are driving towards that higher goal.

Here are examples of some other company BHAGs:

- SAP: "20 by 2015"—20 billion euros in revenue by the year 2015

- Starwood Hotels: 1500 by 2014—1500 hotels by the year 2014

- BioRad: B.I.G.—$5 billion in sales, be independent, be global

- Citizens & Northern Bank: 20/20—$20 share price and $20 million in net profits

- Ansell: 2x in 3y—double revenues in three years

Activity 10.2: How Does Your Company Build Trust and Confidence?

List all the ways your company leaders (the CEO, the president, your boss) share the company goals and strategic focus.

Common Ways to Share Goals and Plans

Many people don't realize all the different ways their company leaders and managers communicate goals and strategies to build trust and confidence in the future. Look at the list below.

1. CEO/leader presentations (speeches, town hall meetings, etc.)

2. Annual reports

3. Company newsletters

4. Company website

5. Company intranet

6. Investor analyst calls or forums

7. Posters in common areas

How many of these items does your company use? Did you forget to include some of these items in the list you created for Activity 10.2?

Be honest with yourself. Is the situation that your senior leaders have never shared the goals of the company, or have they shared them but you just don't remember them?

Be Proactive on Trust and Confidence

If you think more can be done to foster a culture of trust and confidence, talk to your manager about it.

SAMPLE EMAIL TO MANAGER

```
Hi Asha,

I've been thinking lately about this
company's plans for the future and realized
that I don't know as much about our goals as
I probably should. Can we meet sometime in
the next couple of weeks to discuss?
```

Ideas for how you might have a conversation with your manager:

- "I want to make sure I'm clear on our company's priorities and goals. Can you review them with me or point me to where they can be found?"

◆

"A true BHAG is clear and compelling, serves as a unifying focal point of effort, and acts as a clear catalyst for team spirit."

—*Collins & Porras*

◆

- "Can you share your own thoughts on how our department goals align with our company goals?"

- "Asha, can we review my own annual goals again to make sure they align with the bigger picture?"

- "I know the CEO has shared our long-term goals, but I have a hard time remembering them. Can you share them with me again?"

- "Asha, I'd like to make sure I remember our company's long-term goals. Could we work with the whole team to come up with ways to simplify and remember them?"

Do-It-Yourself BHAGs

If you think that more can be done to help yourself and your colleagues remember your organization's long-term goals, and you feel confident that you're making progress towards them, consider what you can do to contribute.

1. Remember the low hurdle we must all step over first: always be honest and transparent.

2. Find your company's goals:

    a. Look on your company's website.

    b. Look through the annual report.

    c. Ask someone!

3. Print the company goals and post the printout in your office.

4. Put the goals in your calendar or notebook.

5. Put the goals in a public area, such as near the coffeemaker.

6. Consider your own goals for the year, or perhaps the goals that are in your performance plan. How do they align with and support the broader company goals?

If your company has long-term goals but has not created a short BHAG, like "2020 Vision," consider doing it yourself. You could work with your team to come up with a catchy phrase for your company's goals, or you could focus on your own department and have a team-level BHAG.

We've come a long way, exploring the key engagement drivers of communication, growth, recognition, and trust. The next chapter is designed to make you feel a little uncomfortable. It will teach you how to handle the disengaged folks in your workplace and give you tools to make sure that you aren't bringing other people down.

CHAPTER 11
Tough Love

"In every life we have some trouble,
But when you worry you make it double,
Don't worry, be happy."
–Bobby McFerrin

We've covered a lot of ground and you're almost done with this book. Hopefully you have a clear understanding of engagement—not just why your company cares about it, but why *you* should care about it for your health and family relationships. If you're feeling engaged right now, then just skip this chapter—why waste time?!

But if you're still not convinced, if you think your situation is hopeless, or if you are surrounded by those who like to wallow in negative feelings, I'm now going to give you a dose of tough love.

Do you remember the character Debbie Downer from the TV show *Saturday Night Live*? Portrayed by comedian Rachel Dratch, Debbie Downer was a character who would bring everybody down with her negative attitude and comments.

In the original skit, Debbie and her family are having a meal at Walt Disney World, and her siblings are excitedly discussing the Disney rides and costumed characters. Throughout, Debbie Downer drops comments about train crashes, terrorist attacks, and the fact that she can't have children. After each negative, out-of-the blue comment you can hear a trumpet's wah-wah sound.

This chapter, in short, is about how to deal with Debbie Downers and how not to be a Debbie Downer yourself at work.

Dealing with Debbie Downer at Work

Even if a company is doing everything right, even if every manager is doing everything right, even if the workforce has been trained in how to be fully engaged, there will be some people who still won't be engaged.

After all, remember the great turnaround success story about Campbell Soup? They had one of the highest engaged-to-disengaged ratios ever, 23-to-1, which means that if Doug Conant gathered 100 people in the room for a meeting, there would *still* be four disengaged people there.

More practically, most companies should be happy with a 10-to-1 engaged-to-disengaged ratio. Again, that realistically means that every 10-person team is likely going to have one disengaged person.

Someone who is always disengaged might just be in the wrong place. Perhaps her parents pressured her into becoming a doctor, but she doesn't like blood and guts! Maybe she truly likes being a lawyer, but she wants to do public advocacy work and not the slip-and-fall cases handled by her current firm. Maybe she loves being a software engineer, but her style is more West Coast sandals than East Coast heels.

Then there are those disengaged people who are happy being unhappy. It's built into their personality. For these folks, they may have been wronged or disappointed in the past and their negativity serves as armor that protects them from being disappointed or hurt again. You can't get bummed out when something doesn't work out when you already know that everything stinks, right? Yep, it's a perverse logic but unfortunately common.

Here are eight steps to deal with the Debbie Downers at work.

1. <u>Don't get dragged down</u>—The old saying is "Misery loves company." The most important thing is to be aware of who the Debbie Downers are in your company and to make sure they don't suck you into their world of negativity. Keep your guard up!

♦

*"God, give me grace to accept
with serenity the things that
cannot be changed,
Courage to change the things
which should be changed, and
the Wisdom to distinguish the
one from the other."*

—Reinhold Niebuhr

♦

2. Listen—It's tempting to just tune these people out, but this rarely stops them. If anything, they'll talk and argue more forcefully because they'll think nobody cares about them. The best thing to do is to use good, normal active listening techniques, as you would for anyone else.

3. Use a time limit for venting—Remember that there is a difference between being a perpetual pessimist and having an occasional need to vent. Everybody has tough times, and sharing our feelings can make us feel better. Use the "5-minute rule" when it comes to this. Let your colleague vent for five minutes, but after that, assume that he's entered Debbie Downer mode, and proceed with the next steps.

4. Don't agree—It's tempting to try to appease Debbie Downer to make him or her stop and go away. As the person complains about benefits or the boss or whatever, you might be inclined to give a little nod of your head or a quiet "yeah" or even a "what can we do?" Even though these responses seem harmless, they just throw fuel on the flames.

5. Don't stay silent—If you are clearly listening but say nothing, Debbie Downer will interpret your silence as agreement. Worse, if others are present, they too will assume that you agree. Whether the complaint is about the boss or the benefits or the

client, silence means you agree with the complainer.

6. <u>Switch extremes into facts</u>—Negative people often speak in extreme terms that match their worldviews. They talk about "never" and "always." Your first goal is to switch them to fact-based statements.

Negative Ned: *Andy is such a slacker! He's never on time for our morning meetings. How are we supposed to hit our deadlines when he's never here?*

You: *Ned, you're clearly frustrated. I seem to remember that Andy was on time at our meetings on Monday, Tuesday, and Wednesday of last week. He was late on Thursday and Friday. So you mean he's late frequently, not always; right?*

7. <u>Move to problem solving</u>—People who whine a lot often feel powerless and believe that the situation is hopeless. Your only chance of ending their negativity is to help them to move into a problem solving mode. This doesn't always work, but it's the only antidote known.

You: *Ned, when Andy is late, it does get us off to a slow start. What do you suggest we do?*

Negative Ned: *Nothing, it's hopeless…*

You: *Why do you say that? Have you tried anything?*

Negative Ned: *What?! What are we supposed to do?*

You: *I don't know, Ned; you don't have any ideas? Like maybe we could talk to Andy?*

Negative Ned: *Like that will really work.*

You: *Look, why don't we just explain that when he's late in the morning, it means we can't lay out the day's priorities, so it slows us all down? Maybe there is something going on in his personal life we don't know about. Maybe he has no idea of the ripple effect he's causing. Maybe he can call in from the road when he's going to be here late.*

Negative Ned: *I guess it's worth a shot.*

8. Cut them off—If, after all your efforts, you deem these people to be hopelessly negative, you need to cut them off. Make sure they aren't just venting for a few minutes, make sure you weren't previously encouraging them, make sure they can't switch to problem solving, and then politely shut them down.

    You: *Dude, can we change the subject? You're really bumming me out. If you want to vent for a couple minutes, fine. If you want me to help you solve the problem, fine. But life is too short to wallow. Let's move on to something else...*

Don't *Be* Debbie or David Downer

You aren't a Debbie Downer or a David Downer yourself, are you?

OK, here comes the tough love.

Are you unhappy at work? Do you think you have a bad boss? How about in your last job—also unhappy and your boss was a jerk back then, too? And what about the job before that? See any patterns here?

If you find that you're always disengaged regardless of the company you're in and whom you're working for, maybe—just maybe—it's you.

Many people who have been mistreated, or who have had bad luck or a bad experience, make universal judgments as a form of emotional armor, so they'll never again be disappointed.

It's the same defense mechanism some people use in relationships. If you've decided that all men are jerks (or fill in whatever negative noun you prefer), then you won't be surprised, disappointed, or hurt when another one shows up. In fact, if that's what you've decided, it's likely that you'll notice all the jerk-like qualities in men you know because doing so supports your theory, and you'll become blind to their good traits.

◆

The happiest people don't have the best of everything, they just make the best of everything.

◆

We need to realize that every organization and every manager is in a constant state of growth and development. Nobody is perfect. There are good traits, and things that need to be improved. Good days and quarters, and bad days and quarters. We need to let go of past wrongs and disappointments.

You might be thinking, "My boss is fine; I just don't like my work. How can I be engaged working as a janitor/assistant/cook/lawyer?"

If you picked the wrong industry or the wrong profession or just the wrong company, do everyone a favor and find a new job. Now that is some "tough love" advice.

I know it sounds harsh, but you aren't doing your employer, your colleagues, or even your family any favors by sticking it out and being miserable at work. And until you *have* found that perfect job and boss, how about trying to make the most of the situation you're in?

Ultimately, think about this: do you want to go through life being known by coworkers, friends, and family as a sad sack—a real "downer"? Or do you want to fill your friends and family and colleagues with optimism, hope, can-do spirit, and humor? Don't you want to be the person that others turn to when *they* are having a bad day?

Four Quick Tips for Happiness

Psychologists who study happiness often recommend that in addition to working on the top drivers of employee engagement, you do some other easy tasks to improve your daily mood.

1. Practice daily gratitude—Don't just notice what is wrong with your life; notice what is right in your life. All you have to do to feel grateful is to watch the stories on the evening news: the war refugees, the unemployed, the homeless and hungry, the ill, the crime victims. Does your bad day at work really seem so awful? I feel like the luckiest man alive whenever I pause for just a few seconds to count my blessings: healthy kids, a home, great fresh food, friends, TV and books for entertainment. Life is good.

2. Exercise—Many research studies have shown that moderate daily exercise can have a big effect on your mood. Whether it's a brisk walk outside during your lunch hour or an early morning jog on the treadmill, physical activity can release brain chemicals called endorphins and lift your mood.

3. Sleep—Happiness researcher and author Gretchen Rubin recommends that getting enough sleep become one of the first things you do to increase happiness. Research shows that it is difficult to get enjoyment from any activity—even watching TV or socializing—if we are tired.

4. <u>Don't worry</u>—be happy, as the song goes. This last common-sense tip is so obvious, but difficult for so many "worriers" out there. Take the advice of the wise Dalai Lama, who wrote:

    "If a problem is fixable, if a situation is such that you can do something about it, then there is no need to worry. If it's not fixable, then there is no help in worrying. There is no benefit in worrying whatsoever!"

Enough with the tough love. Let's wrap it up!

CONCLUSION
Five Daily Questions

"Choose to be optimistic; it feels better."
–Dalai Lama

Amy Wrzesniewski is a Yale University professor who conducts research on people's attitudes about work. One of her key discoveries is that people tend to view their employment in one of three ways:

- <u>As a job</u>—They give their time and work in exchange for money, to take care of the necessities of life.

- <u>As a career</u>—They receive social satisfaction and emotional rewards by advancing, getting bigger and better titles, and moving up the career ladder.

- <u>As a calling</u>—Their work is tied to their personal identity and they believe their labor has meaning and purpose.

Not surprisingly, those people who viewed their job as a calling tended to get greater engagement and satisfaction from their work, regardless of the challenges involved.

Interestingly, these views aren't correlated to income levels or job types. The research suggests that there are as many janitors who view their job as a calling as there are doctors or CEOs. It has nothing to do with the job itself; *it is entirely based on the outlook and attitude of the individual*.

Harvard Psychologist, Timothy Butler, was quoted in *Fast Company* with this explanation:

> *There are three words that tend to be used interchangeably-and shouldn't be. They are "vocation," "career," and "job." Vocation is the most profound of the three, and it has to do with your calling. It's what you're doing in life that makes a difference for you, that builds meaning for you, that you can look back on in your later years to see the impact you've made on the world.*

From the very start, I've said that your company and your manager have a large role to play when it comes to

94

employee engagement. But half the battle is up to you. You can choose your attitude.

You need to be *mindful* of engagement. At the end of every day, ask yourself these questions:

---

5 DAILY ENGAGEMENT QUESTIONS

1. What did I do today to improve communication with my manager and peers?

2. What actions did I take today to learn and grow?

3. Whom did I thank today, and who recognized me?

4. Was I mindful today of our company's long-term goals?

5. Today, how engaged was I at work?

I wrote this book because I'm passionate about the power that employee engagement has to transform organizations and individuals alike.

Life is too short for you to be unhappy at work.

You love your family too much to be coming home stressed, angry, or emotionally drained.

If you follow the simple plan laid out in this book, your good-faith efforts have the power to strengthen your relationship with your manager and to energize your team.

Good luck!

ABOUT

Kevin Kruse

Kevin Kruse is an internationally recognized leadership expert, *New York Times*, *Wall Street Journal*, and *USA Today* bestselling author, and Forbes.com columnist.

As a popular keynote speaker, Kevin has addressed diverse audiences, ranging from *Fortune* 500 companies to non-profits to conferences and even the U.S. Marine Corps.

As a serial entrepreneur, Kevin has built and sold several multimillion-dollar companies that have won both *Inc.* 500 and Best Place to Work awards.

When not busy at his day job, he supports the Acumen Fund and other charities through the Kevin Kruse Foundation.

Kevin can be reached at info@kevinkruse.com and the following sites below:

Website: www.KevinKruse.com.

Facebook: http://www.facebook.com/KruseAuthor

Twitter: https://twitter.com/kruse

LinkedIn: http://www.linkedin.com/in/kevinkruse67

His books include:

- *We: How to Increase Performance and Profits through Full Engagement*

- *Employee Engagement 2.0: How to Motivate Your Team for High Performance (A Real-World Guide for Busy Managers)*

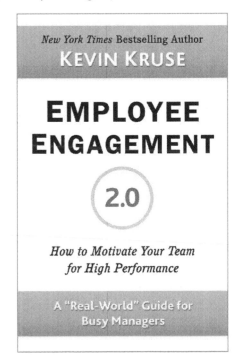

101 Top Engagement Experts

Using Twitter and subscribing to blog posts are great ways to learn more and to stay informed on the latest research and thinking in the area of employee engagement. I encourage you to follow these 101 engagement experts to deepen your understanding of motivation, engagement, and happiness at work.

Erika Andersen
Author, *Leading So People Will Follow*
Twitter: @erikaandersen
Website/Blog: http://erikaandersen.com

Susan Avello
Owner, Social Buzz Concepts

Twitter: @susanavello
Website/Blog: HRVirtualCafe.com

Cheri Baker
President, Emergence Consulting
Twitter: @cheribaker
Website/Blog: http://blog.emergenceconsulting.net

Ann Bares
Consultant/Blogger, Compensation Force
Twitter: @annbares
Website/Blog: http://compforce.typepad.com

John Baldoni
President, Baldoni Consulting LLC
Twitter: @JohnBaldoni
Website/Blog: Lead By Example www.johnbaldoni.com/blog

Irene Becker
Speaker, Coach, Writer, 3Q Leadership Blog
Twitter: @justcoachit
Website/Blog: http://justcoachit.com

Meghan Biro
Founder & CEO, Talent Culture
Twitter: meghanmbiro
Website/Blog: www.talentculture.com

Steve Boese
Twitter: @SteveBoese
Website/Blog: http://fistfuloftalent.com/meet-steve-boese-html

Gary Brose
Author, Motivation Studies
Twitter: @bizsherpa
Website/Blog: www.motivationstudies.org

Dawn Burke
Twitter: @DawnHRrocks
Website/Blog: http://fistfuloftalent.com/meet-dawn-hrdlica-burke-html

Susan Burns
Chief Talent Strategist, Talent Synchronicity
Twitter: @TalentSynch
Website/Blog: www.TalentSynchronicity.com

Alison Chisnel
The HR Juggler
Twitter: @AlisonChisnell
Website/Blog: http://thehrjuggler.wordpress.com

Douglas R. Conant
Founder & CEO, ConantLeadership
Former CEO, Campbell Soup Company
Twitter: @DougConant
Website/Blog: www.conantleadership.com

Lolly Daskal
Founder and President of Lead From Within
A global consultancy Firm that is passionate about Heart Based Leadership
Twitter: @lollydaskal
Website/Blog: www.lollydaskal.com

Kelly Dingee
Twitter: @SourcerKelly
Website/Blog: http://fistfuloftalent.com/meet-kelly-dingee-html

Holland Dombeck
Editor, Fistful of Talent
Twitter: @Holland_Dombeck
Website/Blog: http://fistfuloftalent.com/meet-holland-dombeck

David Ducheyne
Chief People Officer, Securex
Twitter: @dducheyne
Website/Blog: www.Hrchitects.net
LinkedIn Group: Employee Engagement

Kris Dunn
Twitter: @Kris_Dunn
Website/Blog: http://fistfuloftalent.com/2008/05/about-kris-dunn-fistful-o.html

S. Chris Edmonds
Founder & CEO, The Purposeful Culture Group
Twitter: @scedmonds
Website/Blog: http://drivingresultsthroughculture.com

Ron Edmondson
Pastor, Immanuel Baptist Church
Twitter: @ronedmondson
Website/Blog: www.ronedmondson.com

Ben Eubanks
HR Manager, Pinnacle Solutions, Inc.
Twitter: @beneubanks
Website/Blog: http://upstarthr.com

Melissa H. Fairman
HR Generalist, Service Partners
Twitter: @HrRemix
Website/Blog: www.hrremix.com

Brad Federman
President, Performancepoint, LLC.
Chief Operating Officer, F&H Solutions Group
Twitter: @bfederman
Website/Blog: www.performancepointllc.com/blog-0/

Fistful of Talent
Twitter: @FistfulofTalent
Website/Blog: www.fistfuloftalent.com

Joseph Fung
CEO, TribeHR
Twitter: @TribeHR
Website/Blog: http://tribehr.com/blog

Vele Galovski
Author, *Perpetual Innovation Machine*
Twitter: @vgalovski
Website/Blog: Perpetualinnovationmachine.com

Tim Gardner
Director, Organizational Effectiveness, Kimberly-Clark Corp.
Twitter: @TimJGardner
Website/Blog: The HR Introvert, http://thehrintrovert.com

Joe Gerstandt
The Value of Difference
Twitter: @joegerstandt
Website/Blog: www.joegerstandt.com/blog

Gautam Ghosh
Organizations 2.0
Twitter: @gautamghosh
Website/Blog: www.gautamblogs.com

Steve Gifford
Twitter: @BaghdadMBA
Website/Blog: http://fistfuloftalent.com/meet-steve-gifford

China Gorman
China Gorman Blog
Twitter: @chinagorman
Website/Blog: http://chinagorman.com

William Gould
HR Soot
Twitter: @wllmgould
Website/Blog: www.hrsoot.com

Alison Green
Ask a Manager
Twitter: @AskAManager
Website/Blog: www.askamanager.org

Mike Haberman
Senior HR Consultant, Omega HR Solutions, Inc
Twitter: @MikeHaberman
Website/Blog: http://omegahrsolutions.com

Lance Haun
Twitter: @thelance
Website/Blog: http://lancehaun.com

Erika Heald
Editor-in-Chief, Achievers
Twitter: @Achievers
Website/Blog: The Employee Success Blog,
http://blog.achievers.com

Paul Hebert
Vice President - Solutions Design
Twitter: @incentintel
Website/Blog: Symbolist, www.symbolist.com
 http://fistfuloftalent.com/meet-paul-hebert-covering-1-html

Frode Heimen
Customer Service Expert, Kundeserviceskolen as
Twitter: @FrodeHeimen
Website/Blog: http://www.nevermindthemanager.com

Jeremy Henderson
Chief Client Partner, Jungle Red Communication
Twitter: @Jungle_Red_Comm
Website/Blog: www.jungleredcommunication.com
LinkedIn Group: Employee Communications and Engagement

Mike Henry
Sr. Chief Instigator, Lead Change Group, Inc.
Twitter: @mikehenrysr
Website/Blog: http://leadchangegroup.com

John Hollon
Vice President for Editorial and Editor-in-Chief, TLNT
Twitter: @JohnHollon (on Twitter)
Website/Blog: www.TLNT.com

Dierdre Honner
HR Maven
Twitter: @theHRmaven
Website/Blog: www.thehrmaven.com

Michael Hyatt
Intentional Leadership
Website/Blog: http://michaelhyatt.com
Twitter:@michaelhyatt

Derek Irvine
VP Client Strategy & Consulting, Globoforce
Twitter:@DerekIrvine
Website/Blog: http://www.recognizethisblog.com

Charlie Judy
HR Fishbowl
Twitter: @HRfishbowl
Website/Blog: www.hrfishbowl.com

Lola Kakes
Effortless HR
Twitter: effortlessHR
Website/Blog: www.effortlesshr.com

Marisa Keegan
Twitter: @MarisaKeegan
Website/Blog: www.marisakeegan.com &
http://fistfuloftalent.com/105-questions-with-marisa-keegan-html

Barbara Kimmel
Executive Director, Trust Across America
Twitter: @BarbaraKimmel
Website/Blog: www.trustacrossamerica.com

Alexander Kjerulf
Chief Happiness Officer
Twitter: @alexkjerulf
Website/Blog: www.positivesharing.com

Jason Lauritsen
CEO, Co-Founder, Talent Anarchy
Twitter: @JasonLauritsen
Website/Blog: www.talentanarchy.com

Dwane Lay
Author, *Lean HR*
Twitter: @leanhr & @dwanelay
Website/Blog: www.leanhrblog.com

Jessica Lee
Twitter: @Jessica_Lee
Website/Blog: http://fistfuloftalent.com/meet-jessica-lee-html

Victor Lipman
Author, *Management Matters* on Forbes
Twitter: @victorlipman1
Website/Blog:www.psychologytoday.com/experts/victor-lipman

Sharlyn Louby
Author of *HR Bartender*
Twitter: @hrbartender
Website/Blog: www.hrbartender.com

Suzanne Lucas
Evil HR Lady
Twitter: @RealEvilHRLady
Website/Blog: http://evilhrlady.org

David Macleod/Nita Clarke
Engage for Success
Twitter: @engage4sucess
Website/Blog: www.engageforsuccess.org

Paul Marciano, Ph.D.
Author, *Carrots and Sticks Don't Work*
Twitter: @drpaulmarciano
Website/Blog: http://www.paulmarciano.com/category/myblog/

Judy Martin
Founder, WorkLifeNation
Twitter: @judymartin8
Website/Blog: www.WorkLifeNation.com

John C. Maxwell
Leadership Speaker and Author
John Maxwell Company
Website/Blog: http://johnmaxwellonleadership.com
Twitter: @johncmaxwell

Susan Mazza
CEO Clarus Consulting Group, LLC
Twitter: @SusanMazza
Website/Blog: http://www.randomactsofleadership.com

Trish McFarlane
Director, Human Resources, Perficient, Inc.
Twitter- @TrishMcFarlane
Website/Blog: http://hrringleader.com and
http://womenofhr.com

Barrie Mershon/ Linda Brenner
Managing Director, Designs on Talent
Twitter: @DesignsOnTalent
Website/Blog: http://www.designsontalent.com/blog/

Jennifer V. Miller
Managing Partner, SkillSource
Twitter: @JenniferVMiller
Website/Blog: The People Equation, http://people-equation.com/

Jessica Miller-Merrell, SPHR
HR Blogger & Blogging 4 Jobs
Twitter: @_hrblogger
Website/Blog: www.hrblogger.info

Shauna Moerke
HR Minion
Twitter: @hr_minon
Website/Blog: http://hrminion.com

Matt Monge
Chief Culture Officer at Mazuma Credit Union & Chief Mojo
Maker, The Mojo Company
Twitter: @MattMonge
Website/Blog: http://themojocompany.com

R.J. Morris
Twitter: @RJ_Morris
Website/Blog: http://fistfuloftalent.com/meet-r-j-morris

Mike Morrison
Collaboration & Community Leader, RapidBI
Twitter: @RapidBi
Website/Blog: http://rapidbi.com/blog

Shawn Murphy, Speaker and Author
Managing Director at KAI Partners
Co-Founder, Switch and Shift
Twitter: @shawmu
Website/Blog: www.switchandshift.com

Tanveer Naseer
Principal and Founder, Tanveer Naseer Leadership
Twitter: @TanveerNaseer
Website/Blog: www.TanveerNaseer.com

Kate Nasser
The People-Skills Coach(TM), President, CAS, Inc.
Twitter: @KateNasser
Website/Blog: Smart SenseAbilities,
http://katenasser.com/articles

Daniel Newman
CEO, EC3, LLC
Twitter: @danielnewmanuv
Website/Blog: http://millennialceo.com

Jason Pankow
Twitter: @jpankow
Website/Blog: http://fistfuloftalent.com/jason_pankowindex-
html

Kimberly Paterson
Unconventional HR
Twitter: @Kimberly_patt
Website/Blog: www.unconventionalhr.com

Andy Porter
Twitter: @andyt_porter
Website/Blog: http://fistfuloftalent.com/meet-andy-porter-html

Travis Pearl and Kevin Nakao
Amplify Excellence - The MeritShare Blog
Twitter: @meritshare
Website/Blog: blog.meritshare.com

Joey Price
CEO of JumpstartHR
Twitter:@JumpstartHR
Website/Blog: www.jumpstart-hr.com

Skip Prichard
CEO, SkipPrichard.com
Twitter: @SkipPrichard
Website/Blog: www.skipprichard.com

Nisha Raghavan
Co-Host of DriveThruHR- HR's #1 Daily Radio Show
Twitter: @TheHRbuddy
Website/Blog: Your HR Buddy, http://nisharaghavan.com/

Kathy Rapp
Twitter: @KatRapp
Website/Blog: http://fistfuloftalent.com/kathy-rapp-html

Jim Rembach
Chief Spokesman, Beyond Morale
Twitter: @BeyondMorale
Website/Blog: www.beyondmorale.com/blog

Dan Rockwell
Leadership Freak
Twitter: @leadershipfreak
Website/Blog: http://leadershipfreak.wordpress.com

Steve Roesler
All Things Workplace
Twitter: @steveroesler
Website/Blog: www.steveroesler.com

Lisa Rosendahl
Co-Founder and Editor of WomenofHR
Twitter:@lisarosendahl
Website/Blog: http://lisarosendahl.com

Suzanne Rumsey
Twitter: @sbrumsey
Website/Blog: http://fistfuloftalent.com/meet-suzanne-rumsey

Tim Sackett, SPHR
President, HRU Technical Resources
Twitter: @TimSackett
Website/Blog: www.timsackett.com & FOT Blog:
http://fistfuloftalent.com/meet-tim-sackett-covering-talent-and-
technical-recruiting-for-fistful-of-talent-html

Robin Schooling, SPHR
VP Human Resources
Twitter: @RobinSchooling
Website/Blog: HRSchoolhouse.com

Terrence Seamon
Author, *Lead the Way*
Twitter: @tseamon
Website/Blog: http://learningvoyager.blogspot.com &

Dr. William Seidman
CEO, Cerebyte, Inc.
Twitter: @Cerebyte
Website/Blog: http://www.cerebyte.com/journal/

Jappreet Sethi
Human Resources Blog
Twitter: @TopHRblog
Website/Blog: http://humanresourcesblog.in

Jay Shepherd
COO, The Outstandingness Project
Twitter: @jayshep
Website: http://jayshep.com
Blog: Gruntled Employees, http://gruntledemployees.com

Kevin Sheridan
Best Selling Author, Keynote Speaker, & Chief Engagement
Officer
Twitter: @kevinsheridan12
LinkedIn Group: Employee Engagement Emporium

Paul Smith
Director, HR & Operations
Twitter handle: @pasmuz
Website/Blog: www.welcometotheoccupation.com

Meredith Soleau
Twitter: @MeredithSoleau
Website/Blog: http://fistfuloftalent.com/meet-meredith-soleau

Maria Isabel Soto
Talent Sustainability
Twitter: @MarialsabeSoto
Website/Blog: www.talentsustainability.com

Matthew Stollak
True Faith HR
Twitter: @akabruno
Website/Blog: http://truefaithhr.blogspot.com

John Sumser
HR Examiner
Twitter: @johnsumser
Website/Blog: www.hrexaminer.com

William Tincup
Twitter: @williamtincup
Website/Blog: http://fistfuloftalent.com/meet-william-tincup
Michael VanDervort
Human Race Horses
Twitter: @MikeVanDervort
Website/Blog: www.thehumanracehorses.com

Scott Williams
CEO, NxtLevel Solutions
Website/Blog: www.bigisthenewsmall.com
Twitter: @ScottWilliams

David Zinger
Founder, Employee Engagement Network
Twitter: @davidzinger
Website/Blog: www.davidzinger.com

Research
Notes

For readability purposes, this section is intentionally *not* formatted according to MLA guidelines. All sources can be located with easy Google Scholar searches.

Introduction

1. The statement "only 45% of people are satisfied with their jobs" is based on the 2010 Conference Board's annual job satisfaction survey.

2. The statement "only 29% are engaged at work" is based on the Gallup Employee Engagement Index, conducted in the third quarter of 2011.

Chapter 2

1. The statement "Forty-three percent of employee engagement comes from intrinsic motivation" is based

on an IDG Research study made public in 2013. E-mail from IDG Research on file with author.

Chapter 3

1. The statement "People who are dissatisfied at work weigh on average 5 pounds more" is based on "Work Stress and Risk of Cardiovascular Mortality," published by *BMJ*.

2. The statement "People who are unhappy with their bosses are twice as likely to have a stroke" is based on "Managerial Leadership and Ischaemic Heart Disease Among Employees," published in the *Journal of Occupational and Environmental Medicine*.

3. The statement "People who are disengaged at work have less sex" is based on "Work-Family Conflict and Marital Quality," published in *Social Psychology Quarterly*.

Chapter 4

1. The statement "Companies with high engagement scores have customer loyalty rates that are two times higher" is based on "Are they Really On the Job?", published in *Potentials*.

2. The statement "Engaged companies have five times higher total shareholder return" is based on a 2009 study conducted by Kenexa.

3. The statement "Engaged companies have 6% higher net profit margins" is based on a Towers Perrin 2011 study.

4. The Campbell Soup case study and quotes from Doug Conant are based on multiple sources but come primarily from Conant's interview with *Forbes*, published on June 23, 2009.

Chapter 9

1. The statement "Only 10% of adults say thank you to a colleague each day" is based on a 2013 survey conducted by the John Templeton Foundation.

2. The statement "Only 7% express gratitude to a boss" is based on a 2013 survey conducted by the John Templeton Foundation.

Chapter 10

1. The statement "CEO credibility declined 12 points to 38%" is based on the 2012 Edelman Trust Barometer.

Acknowledgments

Thank you, Rudy Karsan and Bill Erickson, for shaping so much of my thinking on leadership and engagement.

Big thanks to my author and publishing friends who provide ongoing encouragement and advice: Erica Andersen, Brad Aronson, Travis Bradberry, Dorie Clark, Jack Covert, Denise Lee Yohn, Paul Marciano, Rajesh Setty, Noel Weyrich, and the entire 800-CEO-READ Author PowWow Posse.

Thank you, Matt Rowe, for the cover design.

Thank you, Catherine Oliver, for copyediting.

Thank you, Chris Couchoud, for the online quiz.

Huge thanks to Christine MacAdams for nailing the final title and advice throughout the project.

Bulk Purchases
and
Speaking Requests

Would you like to give a copy of this book,
Employee Engagement for Everyone,
to all of your team members?

For information on bulk purchases,
or to invite Kevin to speak at your next event,
call 267-756-7089
or e-mail info@kevinkruse.com.

www.KevinKruse.com

19365583R00073

Made in the USA
Middletown, DE
16 April 2015